The Monkey King

Written by Tony Mitton

Illustrated by Mik Brown

Rigby

"Listen," said the monkey king.
"Listen to this funny thing.

If I bang it,
it goes bing.

If I drop it,
it goes dring.

3

If I pat it,
it goes *ping*.

If I tap it,
it goes *ting*.

If I zap it,
it goes zing.

Isn't it
a funny thing?"

Parrot looked.

She flapped her wing.

"King, you are a silly thing!

Can't you see?
Oh, can't you tell?
The thing you have
is just a bell."

Then the king began to yell.
"Come and see. I have a bell!

It makes me want
to dance and sing!

It makes me want
to sway and swing!"

The other birds
began to bring
bits of rotten
fruit to fling.

The birds began
to flap and fling.
The fruit began
to stick and sting.

"That's funny," said
the silly king.
"The birds don't like
the song I sing."